FOUR SEASONS
Art

Written and Compiled by Jean Warren

Illustrated by Barb Tourtillotte

Warren Publishing House
A Division of Frank Schaffer Publications, Inc.
Torrance, California

We wish to thank the following teachers, childcare workers, and parents for contributing some of the ideas in this book: Betty Ruth Baker, Waco, TX; Deborah Balmer, Mesa, AZ; Ellen Bedford, Bridgeport, CT; Sr. Mary Bezold, Corbin, KY; Valerie Bielsker, Lenexa, KS; Janice Bodenstedt, Jackson, MI; Elizabeth M. Bossong, Highland Park, NJ; Cindy Brock, Livonia, NY; Tamara Clohessy, Eureka, CA; Neoma Coale, El Dorado Springs, CO; Jennifer Contaya, Arlington, TX; Marjorie Debowy, Stony Brook, NY; Barbara Dunn, Hollidaysburg, PA; Laura Egge, Lake Oswego, OR; Ann Fair, Uniontown, MD; Marlene Filsinger, Snyder, NY; Rita Galloway, Harlingen, TX; Eloise Gray, San Francisco, CA; Cathy B. Griffin, Plainsboro, NJ; Gemma Hall-Hart, Bellingham, WA; Muriel Hampton, Canfield, OH; Janet Harles, Moorhead, MN; Nancy Heimark, Alamogordo, NM; Cheryl Heltne, Katy, TX; Johanne Hooker, Glendale, AZ; Sally Horton, Waukegan, IL; Barbara H. Jackson, Denton, TX; Wendy Kneeland, Incline Village, NV; Margery A. Kranyik, Hyde Park, MA; Lana Krumwiede, Knoxville, TN; Paula Laughtland, Edmonds, WA; Marilyn Dais Machosky, Westerville, OH; Jacqueline McCracken, Ladysmith, BC, Canada; Kathy McCullough, St. Charles, IL; Judith McNitt, Adrian, MI; Jan Miller, Gatesville, TX; Dawn Picolelli, Wilmington, DE; Beverly Qualheim, Marquette, MI; Jane Roake, Oswego, IL; Sue Schliecker, Waukesha, WI; Betty Silkunas, Lansdale, PA; Kathy Sizer, Tustin, CA; Rosemary Spatafora, Pleasant Ridge, MI; June Stahl, Canfield, OH; Diane Thom, Maple Valley, WA; Margaret Timmons, Fairfield, CT; Jo Urton, Durant, OK; Brenda Valenzuela, Fort Worth, TX; Jane Y. Woods, Sarasota, FL; Suzanne Zasloff, Pittsburgh, PA; Maryann Zucker, Reno, NV.

Managing Editor: Kathleen Cubley
Editor: Elizabeth McKinnon
Contributing Editors: Gayle Bittinger, Susan Hodges
Copy Editor: Mae Rhodes
Proofreader: Kris Fulsaas
Editorial Assistant: Durby Peterson
Book Design/Layout: Sarah Ness, Carol Debolt, Gordon Frazier
Cover Design: Brenda Mann Harrison
Cover Illustration: Marion Hopping Eckberg
Production Manager: JoAnna Brock

ISBN 1-57029-088-1

Library of Congress Catalog Number 96-60130

Printed in the United States of America
Published by: Frank Schaffer Publications, Inc.
          d.b.a. Warren Publishing House

Editorial Office: P.O. Box 2250
          Everett, WA 98203

Business Office: 23740 Hawthorne Blvd.
          Torrance, CA 90505

20 19 18 17 16 15 14 13 12 11 10 9 8 7 6 5 4 3 2

Introduction

Children seem to be born creative. To insure that they keep this natural instinct to create, we need to give them ample opportunities to use safe, open-ended art materials. *Four Seasons Art* is designed as an alphabetical index of art materials, making it easy for you to find ideas for any materials you happen to have available.

Art time is one of the most important parts of a preschooler's day. A few of the crucial things they practice are being creative, solving problems, and developing small-muscle skills. *Four Seasons Art* provides you with developmentally appropriate activities that will help you nurture these and the many other skills practiced and learned through doing art projects.

To help you even further, every page contains an activity suggestion for each of the four seasons. So, if it is fall and you have a supply of wallpaper scraps on hand, just turn to the page titled "Wallpaper" to find an autumn leaf activity you and your children can enjoy starting on right now.

Your children will love these process-centered art projects, and you will love having such a variety of ideas available to you all year-round!

Contents

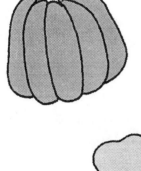

BAKED DOUGH

In a bowl, thoroughly mix together 2 cups flour and ½ cup salt. Stir in ¾ cup water. Knead the mixture for 8 to 10 minutes, until it is smooth and pliable. If the dough is too dry, add a few drops of water. If it is too sticky, add a small amount of flour. Let your children mold the dough into shapes and press on decorations, when indicated. Place the decorated shapes on a baking sheet and bake them at 300°F for about 1 hour, or until hard. Later, spray the painted or unpainted shapes with a clear fixative (in an area away from the children), if you wish.

Fall

Leaf Plaques

Have each of your children roll a piece of dough into a ball and then flatten it into a round or oval shape. Give the children small, fresh leaves to press into their dough shapes. Bake the plaques with the leaves in place.

Spring

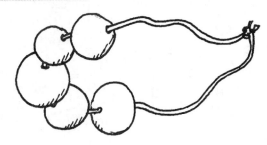

Mother's Day Beads

When making the dough, tint the water with food coloring. Have your children roll the dough into bead shapes. Insert a large nail through each shape before baking. When the shapes have cooled, remove the nails and let the children string the beads to make necklaces.

Winter

Holiday Ornaments

Roll out the dough and let your children cut shapes out of it with holiday cookie cutters. Use a drinking straw to poke a hole in the top of each shape. When the shapes have cooled after baking, let the children paint them with tempera paint and sprinkle on glitter. Tie on loops of yarn for hangers.

Summer

Father's Day Coin Holders

Help your children mold pieces of dough into small bowl shapes. Let them decorate the bowls by pressing on colored pasta pieces and dried beans. Bake the bowls with the decorations in place.

7

BAKING CUPS

Look for packages of multicolored paper baking cups in the baking section of supermarkets. Foil cups and cups with holiday designs may also be available.

 Fall

Thanksgiving Dinners
Let your children glue magazine pictures of foods in the centers of flattened baking cups. Have them glue the flattened cups on paper plates.

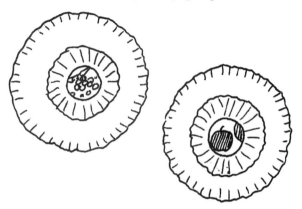

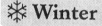 **Winter**

Snowflakes
Flatten baking cups and fold them into fourths. Help your children use scissors to cut notches along the folds. Have them unfold the cups to reveal snowflakes with unique designs.

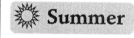 **Spring**

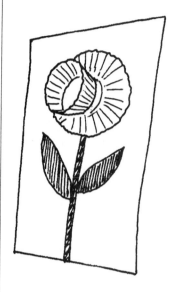

Daffodils
Draw green crayon stems and leaves on pieces of construction paper. Have your children make daffodils by gluing a flattened yellow baking cup at the top of each stem and then gluing a standing yellow cup in the center of the flattened one.

Summer

Butterflies
Let each of your children flatten a paper baking cup and decorate it with crayons or felt tip markers. Show the children how to make a butterfly shape by pinching together the center of the flattened cup. Then help each child twist a pipe cleaner around the pinched center and curl the ends to resemble antennae.

BODY SHAPES

For each of your children, tape a long piece of butcher paper to the floor. Have each child lie on the paper and pose as desired, while you trace around his or her body with a dark crayon. Help the children draw on facial features and other details. Let them decorate their shapes with paint, crayons, or felt tip markers before you cut the shapes out. Display the shapes on a wall or a bulletin board.

☙ Fall

Trick-or-Treaters

Ask your children to tell you about the costumes they would like to wear for Halloween. As you trace around each of their bodies, add details they mention, such as a cowboy hat or a princess skirt.

❀ Spring

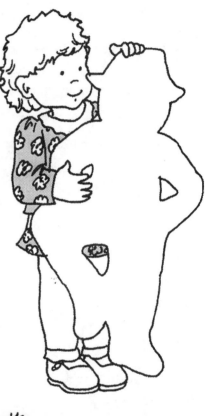

Leprechauns

Before tracing, pose each child on the paper as if dancing a jig. Add a leprechaun hat to each child's shape. Have your children use the colors green and black to decorate their shapes.

❄ Winter

Cold Weather Kids

When you trace around your children's bodies, add details such as mittens, boots, scarves, and hats.

☀ Summer

Beach Bunnies

Draw a bathing suit on each child's shape for him or her to color. Let your children decorate butcher paper "beach towels" to use as a background display for their shapes.

BREAD DOUGH

Purchase frozen whole-wheat bread dough (available at supermarkets). Have your children roll out small, flat pieces. Turn a muffin tin upside down. Help the children mold each bread dough piece over the back of a muffin tin cup. Keeping the dough on the muffin tin, bake according to the package directions to make "edible art" containers. Allow the containers to cool before filling them with snack foods.

 Fall

Thanksgiving Soup Bowls
Place the bread containers in bowls and fill them with turkey or vegetable soup.

 **Winter**

Kwanzaa Cups
Serve harvest vegetables, such as sweet potatoes, carrots, or squash, in the bread containers.

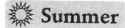 **Spring**

Egg Baskets
Place alfalfa sprouts in the bread containers and top them with spoonfuls of egg salad.

Summer

Summer Fruit Bowls
Fill the bread containers with small pieces of fresh fruits.

CARDBOARD TUBES

Collect a number of cardboard toilet tissue tubes. Longer tubes, such as those from paper towels or gift-wrap, can be cut into shorter lengths, if necessary.

 Fall

Autumn Trees

Give each of your children a toilet tissue tube for a tree trunk and half a paper plate for a tree top. Have the children paint their cardboard tubes brown and decorate their paper plate halves with crayons or felt tip markers in autumn colors. In one end of each tube, cut two slits directly opposite each other. Help the children insert their decorated plate halves into the slits in the painted tubes to complete their trees.

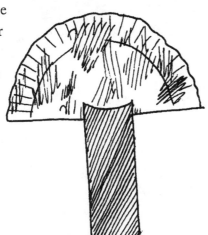

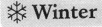 **Winter**

Holiday Bracelets

Collect several cardboard tubes. Cut each tube open lengthwise (so that the "bracelets" will slip on easily). Then cut each tube crosswise into 2-inch-wide rounds. Let your children decorate the rounds with felt tip marker designs and holiday stickers to make bracelets.

Spring

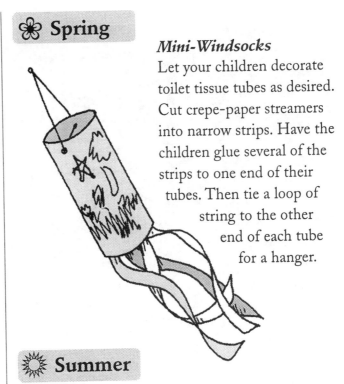

Mini-Windsocks

Let your children decorate toilet tissue tubes as desired. Cut crepe-paper streamers into narrow strips. Have the children glue several of the strips to one end of their tubes. Then tie a loop of string to the other end of each tube for a hanger.

Summer

Goldfish

Have your children cover toilet tissue tubes with 15-inch squares of yellow cellophane. Help them gather the excess cellophane at one end of their tubes and tie it off with string. Have the children fluff out the cellophane to resemble a goldfish tail. Then let them glue black construction paper eyes on their fish.

CHALK

Have colored chalk available—both thin chalkboard chalk and the thick sidewalk variety.

 Fall

Autumn Leaves

Have your children brush liquid starch on pieces of white construction paper for a fixative. Let them color on their papers with red, yellow, and orange chalk. When the papers have dried, cut them into leaf shapes.

❄ Winter

Snow Pictures

Give your children pieces of dark blue or black construction paper. Let them draw on their papers with white chalk to create snow scenes. To keep the chalk from smearing, spritz the finished pictures with hair spray, in an area away from the children.

✿ Spring

Decorated Eggs

Give your children egg shapes cut from white construction paper. Set out colored chalk and small containers of water. Let the children dip the chalk into the water and use it to draw designs on the egg shapes. The water will act as a fixative, keeping the chalk from smearing.

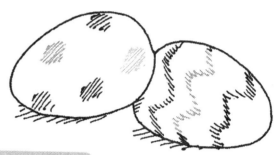

☀ Summer

Sidewalk Art

Provide your children with colored chalk. Invite them to use their imagination to create designs on a cement sidewalk or patio. Let the children use a hose to wash away the chalk designs, or leave them until the next rainfall.

CHEESECLOTH

Mix together two parts liquid starch to one part water. Cut cheesecloth into 4- to 5-inch squares. Let your children dip the squares into the starch mixture, squeeze out the excess, and arrange them in desired shapes. Allow the shapes to stiffen and dry for several hours or overnight. Add decorations, then attach loops of thread for hangers.

 Fall

Ghosts

Let your children drape the wet cheesecloth squares over small, wrapped lollipops to form ghost shapes. Stand the lollipops in an egg carton turned upside down. When the shapes have dried, let the children use a black felt tip marker to draw on eyes.

 **Winter**

Holiday Ornaments

Tint the starch mixture with drops of food coloring. Have your children drape the wet cheesecloth squares over small plastic bottles or similar objects to make freeform ornament shapes. When the shapes have dried, help the children glue on small amounts of glitter.

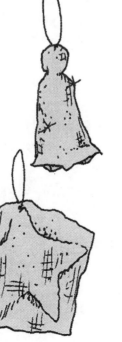

 **Spring**

Butterflies

Add drops of food coloring to the starch mixture. Have your children arrange the wet cheesecloth squares on waxed paper and pinch together the centers to form butterfly shapes. When the shapes have dried, twist a pipe cleaner around the middle of each one and curl the ends to look like antennae.

Summer

Sun Catchers

Have your children flatten the wet cheesecloth squares on waxed paper and squeeze on drops of food coloring. When the squares have dried, hang them in a window.

CLOTHESPINS

Have your children use paint, felt tip markers, or crayons to color wooden spring-type clothespins. Give each child a paper shape to decorate, when indicated. Help the children glue their shapes onto their clothespins. Then let them clip their creations to curtains or other objects around the room.

🍂 Fall

Bat Clip-Ons

Have your children paint their clothespins black to use as bat bodies. Allow the paint to dry. Then give each child a bat wings shape cut from black construction paper to glue onto his or her clothespin.

❄ Winter

Love Bug Clip-Ons

Let your children color their clothespins red. Have them draw faces on small pink construction paper hearts and glue on black paper antennae. Help them glue their heart faces onto the clip end of their clothespins. Then give them each two larger pink construction paper heart shapes to decorate with crayons. Have them glue the tips of the two hearts together to make "wings" to glue onto their clothespins.

❀ Spring

Bird Clip-Ons

For each of your children, cut out a construction paper bird shape about 3½ inches long. Let the children use feathers dipped in paint to decorate their shapes. Then have them glue their bird shapes onto unpainted clothespins.

☀ Summer

Bumblebee Clip-Ons

For each of your children, cut out a bumblebee body shape, about 3½ inches long, from yellow construction paper. Let the children draw black crayon stripes on their shapes and glue on wing shapes cut from white tissue paper. Then have them glue their bee shapes onto unpainted clothespins.

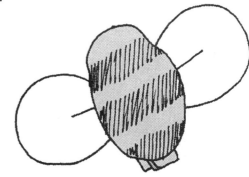

COFFEE FILTERS

Have on hand a number of round, fluted coffee filters—the kind sold for use in automatic coffee makers.

##

Turkey Feathers

Have your children flatten coffee filters and color them with crayons or felt tip markers. Cut turkey shapes out of brown construction paper and add facial features. Help the children fold and tape their decorated coffee filters to the backs of the turkey shapes for feathers.

❄ Winter

Holiday Hang-Ups

Mix food coloring with drops of water in small containers. Let your children fold coffee filters into fourths and dip the corners in and out of the food coloring so that the colors mix and blend. Allow the filters to dry flat. String four or five filters in a row on several pieces of yarn and hang them from the ceiling for decorations.

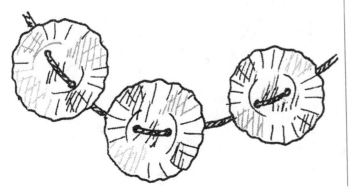

✿ Spring

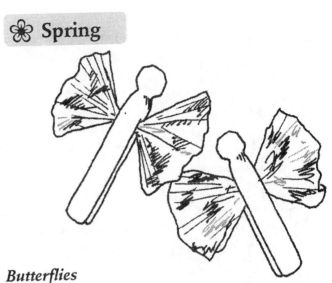

Butterflies

Let your children decorate coffee filters with felt tip markers. Help them spray their filters with water and hang them up to dry. Later, show the children how to pinch the centers of their filters together and slip them inside slot-type clothespins to make butterflies.

☀ Summer

Watermelon Slices

Let your children fold coffee filters into fourths. Have them dip the points of their filters into diluted red food coloring and the edges into diluted green. Unfold the filters and let the "watermelon slices" dry. Later, have the children draw on black seeds or glue on real watermelon seeds.

COTTON BALLS

When gluing cotton balls, help your children keep their fingers clean by providing glue in small bowls. Have your children dip the cotton balls into the glue and then place them on their papers.

🍂 Fall

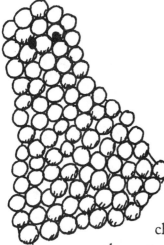

Halloween Ghost

Cut a large ghost shape out of white posterboard. Have your children work together to glue cotton balls all over the shape. Give them two black construction paper eyes to glue on their ghost. Use the ghost as part of a Halloween display on a wall or a bulletin board.

❄ Winter

Snowmen

Help each of your children make a snowman shape by gluing a small white posterboard circle to the top edge of a large circle. Let the children glue cotton balls all over their shapes. To complete the snowmen, have your children glue on black construction paper facial features, hats, and scarves.

✻ Spring

Lambs

Give your children lamb shapes cut from posterboard. Have them glue cotton balls all over their lambs. When they have finished, let them glue on eye and nose shapes cut from black construction paper.

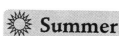

☀ Summer

Sky Writing

Set out a piece of blue butcher paper with a magazine picture of an airplane glued in one corner. Let your children squeeze glue designs on the rest of the paper and cover the glue with stretched-out cotton balls to create "sky writing."

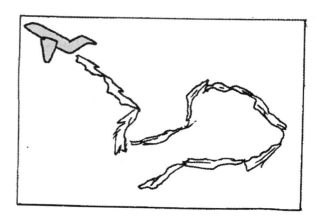

CRAFT STICKS

Have on hand a supply of wooden craft sticks. The sticks can be used plain or they can be colored with felt tip markers, crayons, or paint. To dye the sticks brilliant colors, use a mixture of drops of food coloring and rubbing alcohol.

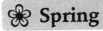 Fall

Autumn Trees

Let your children color craft sticks brown and glue them on pieces of construction paper for tree trunks. Have them draw brown crayon branches growing out from their trees. Then let them glue on small pieces of red, yellow, and orange construction paper for leaves.

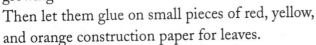

Winter

Star of David Ornaments

Give each of your children six craft sticks that have been dyed yellow. Show the children how to glue their sticks together to make two triangles. Allow the glue to dry. Help each child glue his or her two triangles together to make a Star of David. To make hangers, tie on loops of yarn or ribbon.

Spring

Flowers

Have your children color craft sticks green to use as flower stems. Let them decorate construction paper flower shapes and glue them to the tops of the craft sticks. Anchor lumps of clay in the cups of an egg carton and have your children stand their flowers upright in the clay.

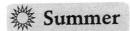 Summer

Popsicle Puppets

From different colors of construction paper, cut out shapes that resemble the frozen part of Popsicles. Let your children use felt tip markers to add faces and other desired details to the shapes. Then help them glue on plain craft sticks for handles. Encourage the children to use the puppets for telling stories.

CRAYON MELTS

Make a frame for each of your children by cutting a seasonal shape out of the center of a piece of dark-colored construction paper. Let each child sprinkle crayon shavings on one half of a piece of waxed paper. Fold the other half over the shavings. Place the folded waxed paper between sheets of newspaper and press with an iron until the crayon shavings have melted. (Close supervision is necessary when using an electrical appliance near children.) Tape or staple the fused piece of waxed paper to the back of the construction paper frame to make a see-through picture.

🦅 Fall

Apples
Make frames in apple shapes. Set out red crayon shavings.

❄ Winter

Bells
Make frames in bell shapes. Provide crayon shavings in holiday colors.

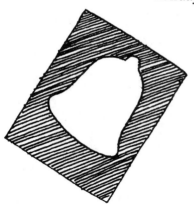

❀ Spring

Shamrocks
Make frames in shamrock shapes. Set out green crayon shavings.

☀ Summer

Flowers
Make frames in flower shapes. Set out crayon shavings in a variety of bright colors.

CRAYON RESIST

On pieces of white construction paper, use a white crayon to draw pictures or designs. (Be sure to press down hard when coloring.) Make a wash of tempera paint and water. Let your children brush the wash over the papers to reveal the crayon drawings.

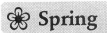 Fall

Ghosts

Draw several Halloween ghosts on each paper. Let your children brush on a black wash.

 Winter

Starry Skies

Draw a number of stars on each paper. Have your children brush on a dark blue or black wash.

❀ Spring

Decorated Eggs

Cut each paper into an egg shape and decorate it with circles, stripes, wiggly lines, and other designs. Let your children brush on a dark pink or purple wash.

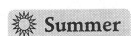 Summer

Undersea Pictures

Draw such items as a fish, a sea star, and a shell on each paper. Have your children brush on a dark blue wash.

CREPE PAPER

Have on hand crepe-paper streamers in a variety of colors. Look for the streamers in craft stores or where party goods are sold.

 Fall

Pumpkins

Give each of your children a pumpkin shape cut from orange posterboard. Have the children color their pumpkin stems with green felt tip markers. Then let them tear and crumple small pieces of orange crepe paper and glue these all over the rest of their pumpkin shapes.

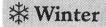 **Winter**

Christmas Tree Ornaments

Provide your children with 6-inch Christmas tree shapes cut from green posterboard. Have the children use brown felt tip markers to color their tree trunks. Let them glue small, torn pieces of green crepe paper all over the rest of their tree shapes. Then help the children brush more glue on top of the crepe paper and sprinkle on glitter. Punch a hole in the top of each shape and tie on a yarn hanger.

 **Spring**

Rainbows

Select crepe-paper streamers in a variety of colors and cut them into narrow strips. Give each of your children several of these strips and half a paper plate. Let the children glue the strips on their plate halves in arcs to make "rainbows."

Summer

Fourth of July Pompons

Cover toilet tissue tubes with red or blue construction paper and let your children decorate them with silver star stickers. Cut red, white, and blue crepe-paper streamers into long, narrow strips. Help the children glue the strips around one end of their tubes to make pompons for shaking.

DOILIES

Look for paper doilies of various sizes in craft stores and stores where party goods are sold.

Fall

Harvest Dinners

Let your children glue magazine pictures of foods on 8-inch paper doilies. Attach the doilies to colored paper plates to display on a wall or a bulletin board.

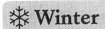 Winter

Valentines

Coat the bottom of a shallow container with red paint. One at a time, have your children place their hands on the paint and then press them on large, white paper doilies. When the paint has dried, let the children glue their doilies to large heart shapes cut from construction paper.

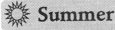 Spring

May Baskets

Let each of your childen decorate the center of a paper doily by gluing on small, crumpled tissue paper squares for flowers. Attach a ribbon or yarn handle to opposite sides of the doily. When the child holds onto the handle, the sides of the doily will curve up to form a "basket."

Summer

Frilly Fireworks

Clip small clothespins to the edges of large and small paper doilies. Let your children hold onto the clothespin "handles," dip the doilies into paint, and then dab them on pieces of construction paper to make prints.

DOT PRINTING

For each of your children, draw a seasonal shape on a piece of white construction paper. Set out new pencils and washable ink pads. Have your children press the pencil erasers on the ink pads and use them like rubber stamps to fill in their shapes with colored dots. Help the children cut out their decorated shapes and glue them on pieces of colored construction paper.

❧ Fall

Autumn Leaves
Draw a leaf shape on each paper. Set out orange and brown ink pads.

❄ Winter

Holly Wreaths
Draw a wreath shape on each paper. Have your children decorate their shapes with red and green dots.

❀ Spring

Kites
Draw a kite shape on each paper. Let your children stamp on dots in bright colors.

☀ Summer

Sea Stars
Draw a sea star shape on each paper. Have your children decorate their shapes with red, orange, or purple dots.

DOTS

Several days before doing a dot activity, let your children start making paper dots. Provide them with a supply of construction paper and construction paper scraps. Let them use a hole punch to punch the dots out of the colored paper.

Fall

Autumn Trees

For each of your children, use a crayon to draw a bare tree on a piece of paper. Let your children brush glue over their tree branches and sprinkle on dots in autumn colors for leaves.

❄ Winter

New Year's Collages

Have your children brush glue on pieces of black construction paper. Let them drop strands of tinsel on their papers and then sprinkle on paper dot "confetti." Display the collages on a wall or a bulletin board for a 3-D effect.

✿ Spring

Decorated Eggs

Let each of your children in turn make designs with glue on a posterboard egg shape. Place the shape in a shoebox with a handful of paper dots. Have the child shake the box and then open it to discover his or her colorfully decorated egg shape.

☀ Summer

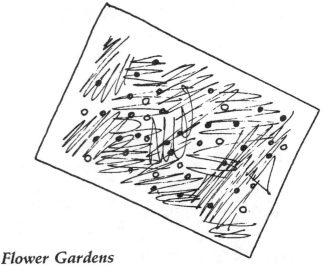

Flower Gardens

Have your children make "gardens" by coloring all over pieces of white construction paper with green crayons. Then let them brush glue on their papers and sprinkle on paper dot "flowers."

FELT

Have on hand various colors of felt squares as well as felt scraps. The squares are available in fabric and craft stores.

🍂 Fall

Quilt

Set out at least 12 felt squares. Let your children decorate the squares by gluing on felt scraps. Using fabric glue or a glue gun, attach the decorated squares in four rows of three squares each to a fabric backing. When the "quilt" has dried, attach loops of fabric to the top and hang it as desired.

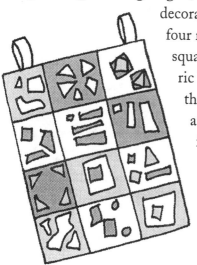

❄️ Winter

Christmas Trees

Let each of your children glue a felt triangle on a piece of posterboard for a tree. Have your children snip felt scraps into little pieces and glue them on their trees for decorations.

❀ Spring

Hats

Give each of your children a hat shape cut from felt. Let the children decorate their shapes by gluing on such items as fabric scraps, lace, ribbon, and yarn. Display the decorated hats on a wall or a bulletin board.

☀ Summer

Fishbowls

For each of your children, use a black crayon to draw a fishbowl shape on a piece of white construction paper. Have the children color in blue crayon "water." Then give each child a fish shape cut from felt to decorate with felt scraps and glue in his or her fishbowl.

FINGERPAINTING

Make fingerpaint by mixing together ¹/₂ cup flour, ¹/₄ cup water, and ³/₄ cup nonconcentrated liquid dishwashing detergent. Add powdered tempera paint or food coloring. Provide pieces of white butcher paper or construction paper for painting.

Apples

Let your children fingerpaint red designs on pieces of construction paper. When the papers have dried, cut them into apple shapes and let the children glue on construction paper leaves and stems.

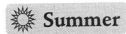 Spring

Flower Pictures

Let your children fingerpaint with pastel colors on pieces of construction paper. While the designs are still wet, give the children flower shapes cut from colored tissue paper to stick on their papers.

❄ Winter

☀ Summer

Undersea Mural

Set out a large piece of butcher paper and let your children fingerpaint blue designs on it. When the paint has dried, hang the paper on a wall and let the children glue or tape on construction paper fish, shells, and seaweed shapes.

Partner Ornaments

Cut large, identical bulb ornament shapes out of butcher paper. Let your children fingerprint designs on the shapes. When the paint has dried, divide the shapes into pairs, tape them back to back, and hang them from the ceiling as decorations.

FOOD PRINTS

Cut fruits or vegetables as indicated to make stamps. Make paint pads by folding paper towels, placing them in shallow containers, and pouring on small amounts of tempera paint. Let your children press the cut surface of the fruits or vegetables onto the paint pads and then stamp them on paper to make prints.

🌿 Fall

Carrot Pumpkins

Cut carrots into thick rounds for stamps and prepare paint pads with orange paint. After making "pumpkin" prints and letting them dry, have your children use green felt tip markers to add stems.

❄ Winter

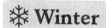

Holiday Gift-Wrap

To make each stamp, press a holiday cookie cutter down into the cut surface of a potato half. Use a small knife to cut away the potato around the outside of the cookie cutter. Remove the cookie cutter and trim off any rough edges of the raised potato stamp. Make a variety of potato stamps and let your children use holiday colors to print wrapping paper and gift cards.

❀ Spring

Flowers

Cut in half such fruits and vegetables as oranges, lemons, carrots, bell peppers, or corn on the cob. Make paint pads in a variety of colors. Let your children use the fruits and vegetables to print "flowers" on pieces of construction paper. When the paint has dried, have the children add crayon leaves and stems.

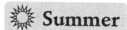
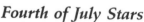

☀ Summer

Fourth of July Stars

Cut apples in half crosswise so that the centers reveal a star shape. Prepare red and blue paint pads. Let your children print the apple "stars" on pieces of white construction paper.

FOOT SHAPES

Have your children take off their shoes. Using a pencil, trace around their feet on pieces of construction paper. Help your children cut out their foot shapes. Then let them add decorations.

 Fall

Ghost Mural
Trace around your children's feet on white construction paper. When the foot shapes have been cut out, have the children use black felt tip markers to draw eyes on the heels. Let them glue their ghosts to black paper to make a Halloween mural.

Spring

Chicks
Trace around each child's foot on a piece of yellow construction paper. After cutting out the foot shape, have the child glue it, toes down, on a piece of white or light blue construction paper. Then show the child how to draw an eye, a beak, and legs on the shape, as shown in the illustration, to turn it into a "chick."

Winter

Footprints in the Snow
Cut several pairs of each child's foot shapes out of black construction paper. Place a piece of white butcher paper on the floor and let your children attach their shapes to make "footprints" on the white paper "snow."

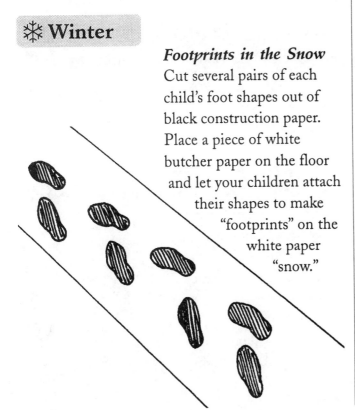

Summer

Butterflies
Cut out each child's right and left foot shape from pink construction paper. Have your children place their shapes toes up side by side, and decorate them with crayons to make "butterfly wings." For each child, use a black crayon to draw a butterfly body, a head, and antennae in the center of a piece of white or light blue construction paper. Then help the children glue their decorated "wings" on their butterfly bodies.

GLUE ART

Have on hand glitter glue, various colors of Elmer's brand decorative color glue, and white school glue in squeeze containers. To make your own colored glue, mix the white glue with tempera paint or food coloring and pour it into clean, empty squeeze containers such as shampoo, hair coloring, or liquid dishwashing detergent bottles.

❧ Fall

Letter Art
Use glitter glue to print alphabet letters or your children's names on index cards. Allow the cards to dry overnight. Let the children place pieces of thin paper on top of the letters or names and color over them with crayons to make rubbings.

❄ Winter

Stained Glass
Let your children use a mixture of black tempera paint and white glue to squeeze designs onto thin white paper such as rice paper. When the glue has dried, have the children paint their papers with watercolors. Hang the papers in a window for the light to shine through.

✿ Spring

Window Garden
Cover the work surface with an old vinyl tablecloth or taped-on plastic wrap. Set out various colors of Elmer's brand decorative glue. Invite your children to squirt the glue onto the work surface to make "flower" designs. (For the best results, the designs should be solid shapes that are not too thick.) Allow the shapes to dry overnight or longer. Carefully peel off the glue shapes and let the children stick them onto a windowpane to make a "garden."

☀ Summer

Father's Day Picture Frames
Give each of your children a picture mat that you have purchased or made from heavy paper. Let the children use white glue tinted with food coloring to squeeze dots, lines, squiggles, and other designs on their mats. When the glue has dried, help the children select pictures to put in their frames.

GREETING CARDS

Collect a variety of old greeting cards. Check with parents or friends to see if they might add to your collection.

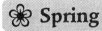 **Fall**

Thanksgiving Placemats

Cut pictures out of greeting cards and let your children glue them on pieces of construction paper. Cover the papers with clear self-stick paper for durability.

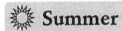 **Spring**

Mother's Day Bookmarks

Cut the fronts of greeting cards into 2-inch-wide strips. Punch a hole at the top of each strip and attach a yarn tassel. Let your children decorate the backs of the strips with crayons or felt tip markers.

Summer

Summer Fun Books

For each of your children, select a greeting card and staple several pieces of plain paper inside it to make a blank book. Let the children decorate the pages of their books with "summer" pictures and designs.

Winter

Frosty Pictures

Mix together equal parts of Epsom salts and boiling water. When the mixture has cooled, let your children use it to paint over the fronts of holiday greeting cards. As the mixture dries, crystals will appear on the pictures.

HANDPRINTS

Spread the desired color of paint in the bottom of a shallow pan. One at a time, let your children place their hands on the paint and then press them on paper to make prints. Or use a paintbrush to coat the children's hands with paint.

 Fall

Turkeys

Using a brush, help your children paint their palms and thumbs with brown paint and their fingers with stripes of red, yellow, and orange. Have them press their hands on paper to make brown turkey bodies with red, yellow, and orange tail feathers. Help them make red finger- prints under their turkeys' chins for wattles. Then let them use felt tip markers to add eyes, beaks, and legs.

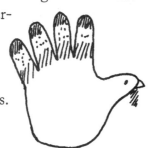

 **Spring**

Birds

For each of your children, use a crayon to draw a bird body on a piece of con- struction paper. Let the children color their birds. Then help each child make one handprint above his or her bird body and one below it for wings.

 **Winter**

Reindeer

For each of your children, draw a brown crayon tri- angle, point down, on a large piece of construction paper. Let the children color their triangles and add eyes and red noses to make reindeer faces. Let them complete their reindeer by making brown handprint "antlers."

Summer

Butterflies

Let one child at a time place both hands in brightly colored paint and make a print on construction pa- per with the fingers of each hand together and the sides of the thumbs touching. When the "butterfly" print has dried, have the child use a felt tip marker to add antennae.

HAND SHAPES

Help your children trace around their hands on construction paper. Then help them cut out their hand shapes. If a large number of shapes are needed, cut them out yourself, through several layers of paper at a time.

 Fall

Turkey Mural

Cut a large turkey shape out of brown paper and attach it to a piece of butcher paper. Hang the butcher paper on a wall. Help your children make hand shapes out of different colors of construction paper. Then help them tape the shapes to the front of the turkey to make the bird's tail.

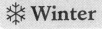 **Winter**

Holiday Wreath

Cut a large donut shape out of cardboard. Help your children make hand shapes in holiday colors. Then help them glue the shapes on the cardboard ring, covering it completely. Add a ribbon bow to the wreath, if desired.

 **Spring**

Little Lambs

Help each of your children make a construction paper hand shape with thumb and fingers outstretched. Turn the shape upside down so that the thumb becomes a lamb's neck and head and the fingers become the legs. Let each child glue stretched-out cotton balls on the lamb's body and a cotton tuft on the lamb's head. Then have the child draw on an eye with a crayon or a felt tip marker.

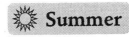

 **Summer**

Palm Trees

Give each of your children a cardboard toilet tissue tube for a tree trunk. Help each child make several hand shapes out of green construction paper for palm fronds. Let your children glue or tape their fronds to the inside of the top of their tree trunks.

LACING

Cut seasonal shapes out of heavy paper and punch holes around the edges. Tie one end of a long piece of yarn to each shape and tape the other end to make a "needle." Let your children lace the yarn through the holes around the shapes. When they have finished, tie off and trim the loose yarn ends.

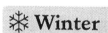 Fall

Footballs

Give each of your children a football shape to paint brown. When the shapes have dried, punch eight holes in each shape along the top edge of the football. Let the children thread white yarn through the holes for laces.

❄ Winter

Christmas Stockings

Let your children lace green yarn around red stocking shapes. Have them add a few holiday stickers for decorations.

❀ Spring

Mother's Day Picture Frames

For each of your children, punch holes around the edges of a clean plastic-foam food tray. Let your children lace yarn through the holes. Then help them glue pictures that they have drawn in the centers of their "frames."

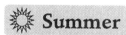 Summer

Canoes

Have your children lace yarn around canoe shapes. Let them decorate their shapes with crayons or felt tip markers.

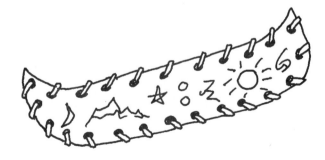

MARBLE PAINTING

Cut construction paper to fit inside sturdy box tops that have been lined with foil. Place marbles in small containers of tempera paint. Have one child at a time place a paper in the bottom of a box top. Spoon one or two paint-covered marbles onto each paper. Let your children tilt the box tops back and forth, rolling the marbles across their papers to create crisscross designs. Remove the papers from the box tops and allow them to dry before adding decorations.

❧ Fall

Spider Webs
Let your children make black designs on white paper. Give them black construction paper spider shapes to glue on their "webs."

❀ Spring

Bird Nests
Let your children make brown designs on white paper. When the paint has dried, round off the corners of the papers to make nest shapes. Give the children construction paper egg shapes to glue in their nests.

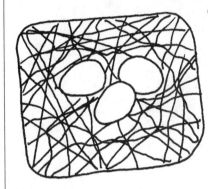

❄ Winter

Snowstorms
Have your children make white designs on dark blue paper. Let them glue on white construction paper snowman shapes.

☀ Summer

Oceans
Have your children make dark blue designs on light blue paper. Give them various colors of construction paper fish shapes to glue in their "oceans."

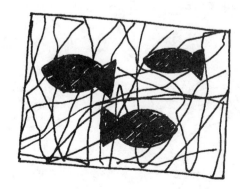

MARBLING

Cut seasonal shapes out of white construction paper. In a shallow pan, mix together 1 cup hot water, 1 tablespoon white vinegar, and 1 tablespoon salad oil. Squeeze drops of food coloring into the pan mixture and swirl them around. Help each of your children in turn dip a paper shape into the mixture and then remove it to reveal a marbleized design. Allow the shapes to dry on paper towels. Then hang them in a window or let the children glue them on construction paper to make note cards.

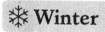 **Fall**

Autumn Leaves
Cut paper into leaf shapes. Use drops of yellow and red food coloring.

 **Spring**

Decorated Eggs
Cut paper into egg shapes. Use drops of any color food coloring desired.

 **Winter**

Hearts
Cut paper into heart shapes. Use drops of red food coloring.

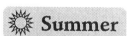 **Summer**

Fish
Cut paper into fish shapes. Use drops of any color food coloring desired.

MILK JUGS

Save plastic gallon milk jugs with lids. Thoroughly wash and dry the jugs, and remove the labels. To add to your collection, ask parents or friends to donate any empty jugs they may have.

 Fall

Trick-or-Treat Containers

For each of your children, cut the top off of a plastic milk jug, leaving the handle intact. Let your children decorate their containers by gluing on construction paper shapes to create "monster faces" and adding glued-on strands of yarn for hair.

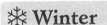 **Winter**

New Year's Hats

For each of your children, cut the bottom part off of a milk jug to use as a hat. (Save the tops of the jugs to use for other activities.) Using a hole punch, punch holes around the edges of the hats. Have the children lace yarn through the holes. Then let them attach stickers for decorations.

❋ Spring

Easter Baskets

For each of your children, cut the bottom part off of a milk jug to use as a basket. (Save the tops of the jugs to use for other activities.) Let the children decorate their baskets by gluing on such materials as cotton balls, paper and fabric scraps, yarn, lace, or ribbon. Punch holes on opposite sides of each basket and attach a thick yarn handle.

☀ Summer

Sand Scoops

For each of your children, cut the bottom part off of a milk jug and put it aside to use for another activity. Glue the lids onto the tops of the jugs to make scoops. Let the children decorate their scoops by squeezing on colored glue or by drawing on designs with permanent felt tip markers.

MOBILES

To make each mobile, hang various lengths of string from a wire coat hanger. Have your children decorate seasonal shapes cut from heavy paper. Attach the shapes to the ends of the yarn pieces. Hang the mobile in a place where the shapes can freely move and revolve.

🍂 Fall

Halloween Mobiles

Let your children use crayons to decorate Halloween shapes such as bats, pumpkins, and ghosts.

❄ Winter

Night Sky Mobiles

Have your children decorate star and moon shapes with silver glitter.

❀ Spring

Spring Mobiles

Give your children flower, bird, and bee shapes to decorate with felt tip markers.

☀ Summer

Beach Mobiles

Let your children decorate fish, sea star, and shell shapes with crayons. Then have them glue on a little sand.

NECKLACES

For necklaces that require yarn or string, use pieces that are about 2 feet long. Knot one end of the yarn or string and wrap tape around the other end to make a "needle." When each necklace is complete, tie the yarn or string ends together.

🍂 Fall

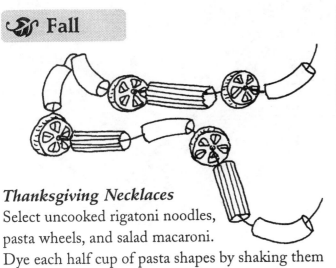

Thanksgiving Necklaces

Select uncooked rigatoni noodles, pasta wheels, and salad macaroni. Dye each half cup of pasta shapes by shaking them in a plastic bag with about ¼ teaspoon rubbing alcohol and 10 drops of food coloring. Lay the pasta on paper towels to dry. Let your children string the pasta shapes on pieces of yarn.

❄ Winter

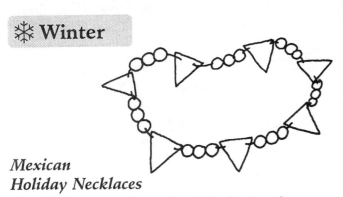

Mexican Holiday Necklaces

Make "tin" shapes by cutting 2-inch triangles out of posterboard and covering them with foil. Punch a hole in each of the two bottom corners of the triangles. To make each necklace, have one of your children string a few beads on a short length of string. Help the child tie one end of the string to a hole in a triangle shape. Tie a another length of string to the other hole in the triangle and let the child string a few beads on it. Continue helping the child in the same manner, adding triangles and stringing beads until the necklace is long enough to fit over the child's head.

❀ Spring

Lei Day Flower Necklaces

Cut 3-inch flower shapes out of various colors of tissue paper. Punch a hole in the center of each shape. Let your children string the tissue shapes on pieces of yarn.

☀ Summer

Dandelion Necklaces

Pick a large number of dandelions and make a slit through each stem close to the stem end. Show each of your children how to gently pull the stem of one dandelion through the slit in another dandelion stem. Then show the child how to pull the stem of a third dandelion through the slit in the second dandelion stem, and so on, to make a chain. When the chain is long enough for a necklace, help the child fasten the two ends of his or her chain together.

OBJECT PAINTING

Mix the desired color of paint and pour it into shallow containers. Then set out paper and the objects needed for painting.

🍂 Fall

Spider Webs

Tie short pieces of yarn onto plastic spider rings (available at discount stores at Halloween). Let your children put on the rings, dip the yarn pieces into black paint, and move the yarn back and forth across pieces of construction paper to make "webs." Later, give each child a small black pompon to glue on his or her paper for a spider.

❄ Winter

Evergreen Designs

Set out short sprigs of evergreens (available at Christmas tree lots) and green paint. Let your children use the evergreen sprigs like brushes to paint designs on construction paper. When the paint has dried, staple the children's sprigs to their paintings.

✿ Spring

Birds

Let your children use feathers to brush blue or brown paint on construction paper bird shapes. When they have finished, let them glue their feathers on their birds.

☀ Summer

Fireworks

Set out red, yellow, and white tempera paint. Have your children dip sprigs of parsley or dillweed into the paint and press them on dark-colored construction paper to make prints.

PAPER BAGS

Have on hand plain paper lunch bags. The bags are available in the paper goods section of supermarkets.

Fall

Pumpkins

Let your children stuff paper lunch bags with crumpled pieces of newspaper. Close the bags with twist ties. Have the children paint their bags orange to make pumpkins. Then have them paint the parts of their bags above the twist ties green for stems.

❄ Winter

Holiday Gift Bags

Let your children tear or cut small pictures out of holiday gift-wrap. Have them glue the pictures on paper lunch bags. Then punch two holes through the top edges of each bag and insert a yarn or ribbon tie. Use the bags to hold holiday gifts.

✽ Spring

Bird Nests

Let your children decorate the sides of brown paper lunch bags with crayons. Help them fold down the sides of their bags to form "nests." Have the children fill the nests with items that birds might use for nest building, such as twigs and pieces of string. Let the children place the nests outside for the birds to discover. Or hang the nests from a tree branch with pieces of ribbon.

☀ Summer

Picnic Bags

Give your children paper lunch bags to decorate with crayons, felt tip markers, or rubber stamps. Let them use their bags for packing lunches before going outdoors for a picnic.

PAPER CHAINS

Cut strips, about 2 by 9 inches, out of construction paper. Give each of your children several of the strips and some glue. (Or, provide them with small pieces of tape.) Show the children how to glue the ends of one paper strip together to make a loop. Next, demonstrate how to make a chain by inserting one paper strip at a time through a loop and then gluing the ends together.

🍂 Fall

Halloween Chain

Let your children make an orange and black paper chain. Give them Halloween stickers to attach to the chain loops for decorations.

❄ Winter

Holiday Chains

At the beginning of December, have your children make a blue and white chain for Hanukkah, a red and green chain for Christmas, or a red, green, and black chain for Kwanzaa. Have them include one loop for each day remaining until the holiday begins. Each morning, let a child remove one loop. Together, count the loops that are left to see how many more days there are before the holiday arrives.

✱ Spring

Caterpillars

Let each of your children use any color of construction paper to make three separate paper loops. Help each child place a drop of glue on the outside surface of each loop. Then help him or her form a "caterpillar" by sticking the loops together in a row. Give the child construction paper eyes and antennae to glue onto the caterpillar.

☀ Summer

Ocean Waves

Hang a piece of butcher paper on a wall. Let your children make chains using strips of blue construction paper. Attach the chains to the butcher paper in wavy lines, one beneath the other, to form an "ocean." Help the children tape or glue several construction paper boat shapes above the waves.

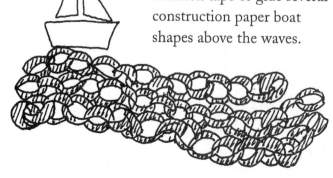

PAPER CUPS

Have on hand small and medium-sized paper cups. If possible, use those that have no decorations.

Fall

Autumn Nature Baskets

Let your children decorate small paper cups by gluing on torn pieces of red, yellow, and orange tissue paper. Attach a pipe cleaner handle to each cup to make a "basket." Have the children use their baskets to hold small nature items such as dried seed pods, twigs, and tiny pine cones.

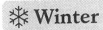

❄ Winter

Groundhog Puppets

Give your children small groundhog faces cut from brown construction paper. Let them glue on thin pieces of cotton for fur, and black construction paper eye and nose shapes. Attach the groundhog faces to the tops of craft sticks to make puppets. Give each child a small paper cup, with a slit cut in the bottom, to decorate with brown crayons. Show the child how to push his or her craft stick puppet down into the cup through the slit. Then demonstrate how to move the craft stick up and down to make the groundhog appear and disappear.

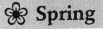 Spring

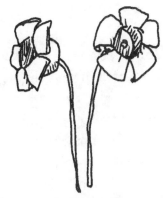

Flowers

Let your children use crayons to decorate the inside and outside surfaces of small paper cups. Using scissors, make five or six cuts down each cup, to about 1 inch from the bottom. Curl the edges of the cut strips over and out to form "petals." To complete each flower, poke the end of a pipe cleaner up through the bottom of the cup and twist it into a knot.

☀ Summer

Fourth of July Hats

Give each of your children a medium-sized white paper cup to use as a hat. Let the children decorate their hats by gluing on red and blue yarn pieces and silver star stickers. Let them glue cotton balls on the tops of their hats. Attach yarn to the sides of each hat for ties.

41

PAPER PLATES

For these activities, use lightweight paper plates with fluted edges.

🍂 Fall

Totem Pole

Have each of your children draw or glue a picture of an animal face on a paper plate. Then tape the plates to a wall in a column to make a "totem pole."

❄️ Winter

Holiday Wreaths

Cut the centers out of paper plates and save them for another use. Give each of your children a paper plate rim. Let the children glue crumpled green tissue paper squares all over their plate rims to represent holly leaves. Then have them glue on a few crumpled red tissue paper squares for berries. Attach yarn or ribbon loops for hangers.

🌸 Spring

Umbrellas

Select paper plates for your children to use to make "umbrellas." With a black crayon, draw a small circle on the back of each plate for an umbrella tip. Let the children paint brightly colored designs on the backs of the plates to complete the umbrellas. To display, attach the umbrellas to a wall or a bulletin board with a pair of construction paper boot shapes peeking out from beneath each one.

☀️ Summer

Sunflowers

Give each of your children a paper plate. Let the children glue sunflower seeds all over the center of their plates. Then give them large triangles cut from yellow construction paper or tissue paper to glue around the rim of their plates for petals.

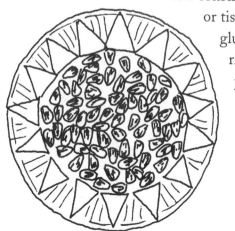

PASTA SHAPES

Look in supermarkets for packages of uncooked pasta shapes, such as macaroni, wagon wheels, bow ties, and corkscrews.

 Fall

Pumpkins

For each of your children, cut a pumpkin shape out of posterboard. Let the children glue pasta shapes all over their pumpkins. When the glue has dried, have the children paint their shapes orange. For hangers, punch holes in the shapes and tie on loops of yarn.

 **Spring**

Mother's Day Tissue Boxes

Give each of your children an unopened facial tissue box. Let the children glue pasta shapes all over their boxes except for the opening on top. When the glue has dried, spray paint the boxes gold in an area away from the children.

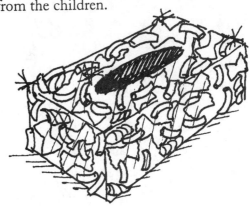

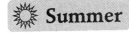 **Summer**

Beaches

Give your children pieces of light blue construction paper. Let them brush glue on their papers and sprinkle on salt for sand. Then let them glue pasta shells on their "beaches."

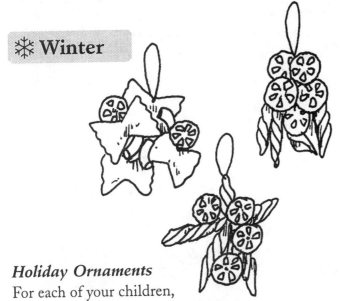

 Winter

Holiday Ornaments

For each of your children, tape a piece of waxed paper to a tabletop. Set out glue and a variety of pasta shapes. Let the children each choose several shapes and glue them together on top of the waxed paper to make ornaments. When the ornaments have dried, peel off the waxed paper and attach yarn hangers.

PHOTOS

Take a head shot photograph of each of your children. Have several photocopies made of each photograph. For each child, cut a desired shape out of white posterboard. Cut out a face hole in each shape. Let the children decorate the shapes. Then tape a copy of each child's photo to the back of his or her shape so that the face appears in the face hole. Use the shapes for bulletin board displays.

🍂 Fall

Trick-or-Treaters

Give each of your children a child shape with a face hole cut out of leave the head. Let the children decorate their shapes by gluing on collage materials for "costumes." Make a Halloween scene with the "trick-or-treaters."

❄ Winter

Snowmen

Give each of your children a snowman shape with a face hole cut out of the head. Have the children decorate their snowmen by gluing on cotton. Use the shapes to make a winter scene.

❀ Spring

Flowers

Give each of your children a flower shape with a face hole cut out of the center. Let the children decorate the flowers by gluing on colored paper scraps. Make a spring "garden" by attaching the flowers to the tops of construction paper stems on a wall or a bulletin board.

☀ Summer

Vacation Cars

Give each of your children a car shape with a face hole cut in the passenger-side window. Have the children color their shapes with crayons or felt tip markers. Use the shapes to make a summer on-the-road scene.

PLACEMATS

When making placemats from construction paper, use the 9-by-12-inch size. If you want the placemats to last, laminate them or cover them with clear self-stick paper.

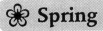 Fall

Thanksgiving Placemats

Give your children pieces of orange, yellow, or brown construction paper. Let them glue on magazine pictures of fruits and vegetables.

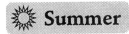 Spring

Shamrock Placemats

Give each of your children a piece of white or light green construction paper. Let the children decorate their papers with green crayon or felt tip marker designs and shamrock stickers.

Summer

Fourth of July Placemats

Set out pieces of blue construction paper. Have your children decorate the papers by gluing on red and white construction paper strips any way they wish. Then let them add silver star stickers.

Winter

Valentine Placemats

For each of your children, cut two placemat-size ovals out of clear self-stick paper and remove the backing from one oval. Let each child place hearts cut from pink, red, and white tissue paper on the sticky oval and sprinkle on glitter. Complete the placemat by removing the backing from the child's second oval and carefully placing it sticky-side down over the decorated oval.

PLASTIC-FOAM SHAPES

Set out clean plastic-foam food trays and metal cookie cutters. Let your children press the cookie cutters into the trays to make outlines of seasonal shapes. Help the children cut out the shapes with scissors. Have them decorate the shapes, first on one side, then on the other. When they have finished, punch a hole in the top of each shape and insert yarn to make a hanger. Use the shapes as room decorations or as parts of mobiles.

Fall

Turkeys
Let your children make turkey shapes with turkey cookie cutters. Have them paint their shapes with Thanksgiving colors.

Winter

Holiday Ornaments
Have your children use holiday cookie cutters to make shapes. Let them brush glue on their shapes and sprinkle on various colors of glitter.

Spring

Shamrocks
Let your children make shapes with shamrock cookie cutters. Have them brush glue on their shapes and sprinkle on green glitter.

Summer

Fish
Have your children use fish cookie cutters to make fish shapes. Let them decorate their shapes by gluing on torn pieces of colored tissue paper.

PLAYDOUGH

To make playdough, mix together 1 cup flour, ¹/₂ cup salt, 6 to 7 tablespoons water, and 1 tablespoon vegetable oil. Add drops of food coloring, or mix the dough with powdered tempera paint for more brilliant colors. Store the playdough in the refrigerator in an airtight container.

🍂 Fall

Thanksgiving Dinners
Let your children use cookie cutters, kitchen gadgets, or their hands to make "foods" with the playdough. Have them place their creations on small paper plates.

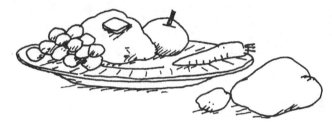

❄ Winter

Holiday Dough
Add powered cinnamon to the playdough, or sprinkle glitter on a table and let your children work it into pieces of playdough.

❀ Spring

Egg Baskets
Set out playdough in a variety of colors. Let your children use the dough to make little baskets filled with colored "eggs."

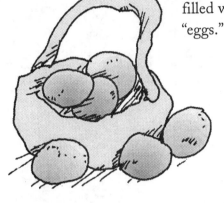

☀ Summer

Sunny Yellow Dough
Color the playdough yellow. Set out all yellow plastic cookie cutters for your children to use with the dough.

PRINTS

Assemble the objects needed for making prints. Then set out the kind of paint required for each activity.

Leaf Prints

Let each of your children paint the vein side of a fresh leaf with water-based fabric paint. Have each child lay the leaf paint-side down on a piece of fabric. Place a newspaper on top of the leaf and roll over it with a rolling pin. Have the child remove the leaf to reveal the print on the fabric.

❄ Winter

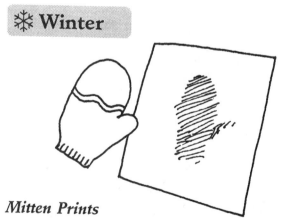

Mitten Prints

Set out old, mateless mittens. Place sponges in shallow containers and pour on tempera paint. Let your children put on the mittens and press their hands first on the paint-covered sponges, then on large pieces of paper to make prints.

❀ Spring

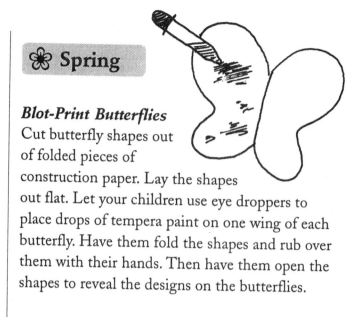

Blot-Print Butterflies

Cut butterfly shapes out of folded pieces of construction paper. Lay the shapes out flat. Let your children use eye droppers to place drops of tempera paint on one wing of each butterfly. Have them fold the shapes and rub over them with their hands. Then have them open the shapes to reveal the designs on the butterflies.

☀ Summer

Cardboard Flower Prints

Cut strips of corrugated cardboard into desired lengths. Roll each piece tightly and secure it with masking tape. Make paint pads by placing folded paper towels in shallow containers and pouring on tempera paint. Let your children dip the ends of the cardboard rolls into the paint and press them on paper to make "flower" prints.

RICE

Select long-grain rice. To dye the rice, shake it in a clear plastic bag with drops of food coloring and rubbing alcohol. Use more of the rubbing alcohol to make a light shade, such as pink, and less of it to make darker shades. Spread the rice out on paper towels to dry. Let your children tear brown construction paper into strips and glue them on pieces of light blue construction paper to make trees with branches. Then let them brush glue around their tree branches and sprinkle on the rice.

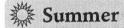 Fall

Fall Trees

Dye the rice orange by mixing together drops of red and yellow food coloring. Have your children cover their tree branches with the rice "leaves," and sprinkle some on the ground below the tree, too.

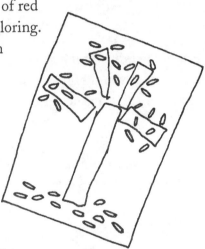

 Spring

Spring Trees

Dye the rice pink and have your children glue it on their tree branches to represent blossoms.

Summer

Summer Trees

Give your children rice that has been dyed green to glue on their tree branches for summer leaves.

Winter

Winter Trees

Let your children glue plain white rice on their tree branches for snow.

RUBBER STAMPS

Collect rubber stamps as needed for each activity. Set out water-based ink pads, or make paint pads by placing folded paper towels in shallow containers and pouring on small amounts of tempera paint.

🍂 Fall

Totem Poles

Give each of your children a narrow strip of construction paper. Set out several different animal stamps and various colors of ink pads. Let the children start at the top of their paper strips and stamp animal prints all the way down.

❄ Winter

Holiday Cards

Set out ink pads in holiday colors and rubber stamps of any kind. Give your children folded pieces of white construction paper for cards. Let them cover the backs and fronts of the cards with stamped-on prints.

❀ Spring

Farm Animal Scenes

For each of your children, draw a simple barnyard picture, including such things as a barn and a fence, on a piece of construction paper. Set out farm animal rubber stamps and ink pads. Let the children use the stamps to make animal prints on their their barnyard pictures.

☀ Summer

Fishbowls

For each of your children, draw the outline of a fishbowl on a piece of light blue construction paper. Set out ink pads and rubber stamps in fish shapes. Let your children use the stamps to fill their fishbowls with fish prints.

SCISSOR FUN

Provide your children with safe scissors and the paper needed for each activity. If necessary, help the children to use the scissors at first.

 ### Fall

Autumn Leaves
Give each of your children a large leaf shape cut from construction paper. Set out colorful scraps and let the children snip them into tiny pieces. Then have them glue the pieces on their leaf shapes.

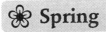 ### Spring

Flowers
Give your children paper baking cups. Let them snip the cups from the outside edge inward. Then have them flatten the cups to form "flowers."

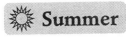

 ### Winter

Evergreen Branches
For each of your children, fold a piece of green construction paper lengthwise. Starting at one end of the paper, draw equally spaced lines from the open edge halfway across the paper toward the fold. Have each child cut the paper just to the end of each line. Then let the child open the paper and decorate his or her "evergreen branch" with circle sticker "ornaments."

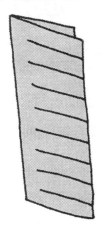 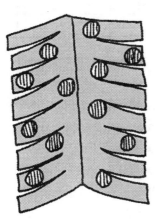

Summer

Suns
Set out paper plates and yellow crayons or felt tip markers. Let your children color the plates. Then have them cut slits in the plates from the outer edge to the center to make "rays."

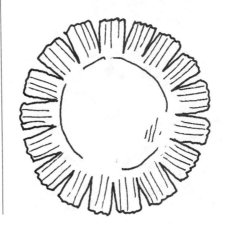

51

SPONGES

Collect sponges and prepare them as needed. Set out tempera paint in shallow containers.

🍂 Fall

Jack-O'-Lanterns

Cut sponges into triangles. Let your children dip the sponge triangles into black paint and press them on orange construction paper pumpkin shapes to make jack-o'-lantern faces.

❄ Winter

Snowy Skies

Cut small circles out of sponges. Give your children the sponge circles and white tempera paint. Let them press the sponges into the paint, then onto blue construction paper to represent falling snowflakes.

✾ Spring

Blossoms

Set out sponge dish mops (the kind sold at supermarkets for washing drinking glasses) and paint in pastel colors. On a piece of butcher paper, draw stems with a green crayon. Let your children press the dish mops into the paint, then onto the paper to print "blossoms" all over the stems.

☀ Summer

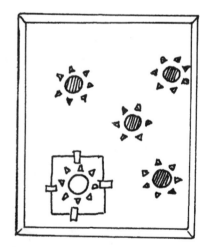

Sunny Windows

Make stencils by cutting sun shapes in pieces of cardboard. Tape the stencils to windows and let your children sponge-paint over them with yellow paint. Wait until the paint has dried before removing the stencils.

TEXTURE PAINTING

Give each of your children a piece of white construction paper, a paintbrush, and a container of paint. Let the children brush the paint on their papers any way they wish to make designs. While the paint is still wet, have them sprinkle on texture material.

🍂 Fall

Leaf Textures
Give your children brown paint and let them sprinkle on crushed dried leaves.

✻ Spring

Flower Textures
Give your children pink paint and have them sprinkle on crushed straw flowers or dried pink flower petals.

☀ Summer

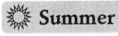

Grass Textures
Let your children paint green designs and sprinkle on grass clippings.

❄ Winter

Glitter Textures
Have your children make designs with white paint and sprinkle on white glitter.

THUMBPRINTS

Set out water-based ink pads, or make paint pads by placing folded paper towels in shallow containers and pouring on small amounts of tempera paint. To make prints, have your children press their thumbs (or fingers) on the stamp pads, then on pieces of construction paper.

🍂 Fall

Autumn Trees

For each of your children, use a brown crayon to draw a bare tree on a piece of white construction paper. Let the children make red and yellow thumbprints on the tree branches and under their trees for leaves.

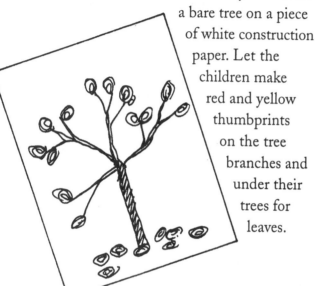

❄ Winter

Snowflakes

Use white tempera paint to make paint pads. Have your children make white thumbprints on blue construction paper for falling snow.

✽ Spring

Egg Baskets

Give each of your children a basket shape cut out of light-colored construction paper. Let the children fill their baskets with various colors of thumbprint "eggs."

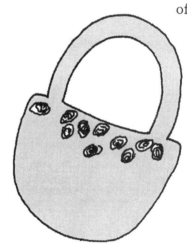

☀ Summer

Bugs

Let your children make black thumbprints on light-colored construction paper. Using a black fine point marker, help them add legs to their prints to create bugs.

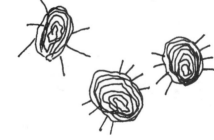

TISSUE PAPER

Have on hand tissue paper in a variety of colors. (Look for colored tissue paper in art or craft stores.) Cut shapes from several layers of tissue at a time when a large number is needed.

🍂 Fall

Leaf Pictures

Cut leaf shapes out of red and yellow tissue paper. For each of your children, collect several stems from real leaves. Let the children place a few tissue leaves on pieces of construction paper and brush over them with diluted glue, allowing the leaves to wrinkle and fold. Then have the children glue the stems on their leaves.

❄ Winter

Vinegar Hearts

Give each of your children a piece of white construction paper and several small heart shapes cut from red tissue paper. Have the children brush white vinegar on their papers and then lay on the red hearts. As the vinegar dries, the tissue paper will fall off, leaving red heart prints.

✿ Spring

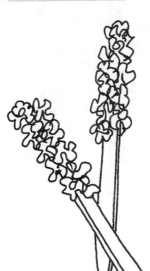

Lilacs

Cut purple and lavender tissue paper into 2-inch squares. Help your children make "lilac blossoms" by twisting one tissue square at a time around the eraser end of a pencil. Let the children use cotton swabs to glue their blossoms to craft sticks.

☀ Summer

Poppies

For each of your children, cut a circle for a poppy center out of black construction paper and five circles for petals out of bright orange tissue paper. Have the children glue the tissue petals around the edge of their construction paper centers, overlapping them as necessary. Then let the children turn their poppies over and glue black beans on the centers.

TORN PAPER

Collect scraps and whole pieces of construction paper. Let your children tear the paper into small pieces. Give the children seasonal shapes cut out of posterboard, if called for. Have the children glue the torn paper pieces all over the shapes. Then let them add other details as needed.

🍂 Fall

Apples

Have your children cover small paper plates with red torn paper pieces. Let them add green construction paper stems and leaves to their "apples."

❄ Winter

Snowmen

Let your children cover snowman shapes with white torn paper pieces. Give the children black construction paper eye, mouth, and hat shapes to glue on their snowmen.

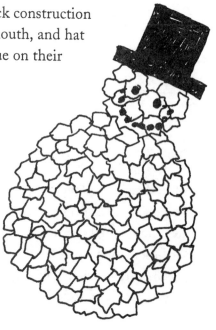

❀ Spring

Kites

Give your children kite shapes to cover with torn paper pieces in bright colors. Let them glue on pieces of yarn for tails.

☀ Summer

Suns

Have your children glue yellow torn paper pieces on small paper plates to make suns. Give them strips of yellow construction paper to glue around the edge of their suns for rays.

WALLPAPER

Collect prepasted wallpaper samples or scraps. (Check wallpaper or hardware stores for free samples or outdated wallpaper books.) Prepare papers as needed for each activity. Set out shapes cut from the wallpaper along with sponges placed in shallow containers of water. To glue on the prepasted shapes, have your children first press them on the wet sponges and then place them on their papers. (Provide white glue if any of the shapes do not adhere to construction paper.)

🍂 Fall

Leafy Branches

For each of your children, use a crayon to draw a tree branch on a piece of white or light blue construction paper. Cut leaf shapes out of wallpaper and let the children paste them on their tree branches.

❄ Winter

Quilts

For each of your children, select a piece of colored construction paper, cut it into a 9-inch square, and then fold it into small squares. Cut wallpaper into matching-size squares. Let your children paste the wallpaper squares to the squares on the papers, making "patchwork quilts."

❀ Spring

Flowers

For each of your children, use a crayon to draw stems and leaves on a piece of white or light blue construction paper. Give the children flower shapes cut from wallpaper. Let them paste the shapes at the top of the stems on their papers.

☀ Summer

Laundry on the Line

For each of your children, use a crayon to draw a clothesline on a piece of light blue construction paper. Cut clothing shapes out of wallpaper. Let your children paste the shapes on their clotheslines as if hanging them out to dry.

WAXED PAPER

Have your children tear colored tissue paper into small pieces. Pour salad oil into shallow containers and set out cotton balls. Give each child a large seasonal shape cut from waxed paper. Let the children use the cotton balls to brush the oil over their waxed paper shapes. Then have them cover their shapes with the small tissue paper pieces. The oil will help the tissue paper adhere to the shapes while making the color translucent.

Fall

Pumpkins

Give your children waxed paper pumpkin shapes. Let them press on orange tissue paper pieces.

Spring

Shamrocks

Provide your children with waxed paper shamrock shapes. Let them press on green tissue paper pieces.

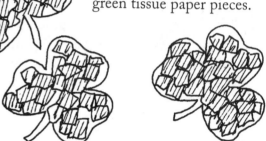

Summer

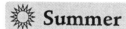

Fish

Cut fish shapes out of waxed paper. Let your children press on tissue paper pieces in any color they wish.

Winter

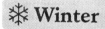

Hearts

Cut heart shapes out of waxed paper. Have your children press on red tissue paper pieces.

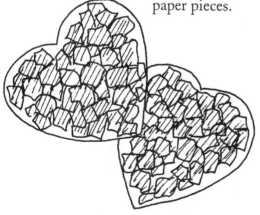

WEAVING

Assemble the materials needed for each activity. As your children begin, help them with their weavings, as needed.

🍂 Fall

Autumn Weavings

Make a loom for each of your children by cutting five notches in each end of a plastic-foam food tray and stringing brown or tan yarn through the notches. Tape the yarn ends to the back of the tray. Show the children how to use the over-under method to weave such items as dried grass, twigs, feathers, and short yarn pieces on their looms.

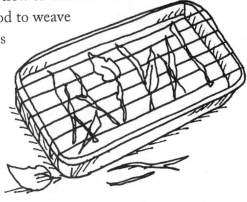

❄ Winter

Kwanzaa Placemats

For each of your children, fold a 9-by-12-inch piece of black construction paper in half lengthwise and cut slits, 1 inch apart, from the fold to within 2 inches of the loose edges. Open the papers and give them to the children. Cut 1-by-9-inch strips from red and green construction paper. Show the children how to weave the strips in and out of the slits in their papers to make woven placemats.

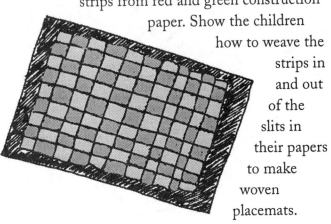

✿ Spring

Bird Nest Bags

Collect one or more citrus bags and cut cotton yarn or string into short pieces. Let your children work in groups or individually to loosely weave the yarn pieces through the holes in the citrus bags. When they have finished, hang the bags outdoors and watch for birds to take the yarn pieces for their nests.

☀ Summer

Berry Baskets

For each of your children, tie a long piece of yarn to a plastic berry basket. Let the children weave the yarn pieces in and out of the basket holes. If desired, let them also weave in items such as ribbon pieces, pipe cleaners, or twine.

YARN

Have on hand colored yarn as needed for each activity. Yarn scraps can be tied together to make longer pieces, if necessary.

🍂 Fall

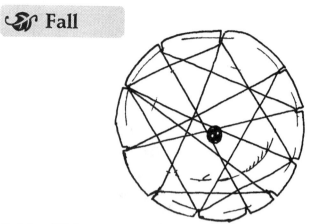

Spider Webs

For each of your children, cut slits around the edge of a sturdy paper plate. Tape one end of a long piece of black yarn to the front. Have each child wind the yarn back and forth across the back of the plate, passing it through a slit each time, to make a "web." When the child has finished, let him or her glue on a black button for a spider.

❄ Winter

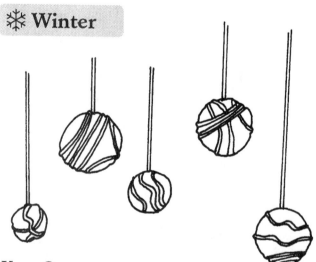

Yarn Ornaments

Collect plastic-foam balls and scraps of colored yarn. Tape one end of a yarn piece to the top of each ball. Have your children spread glue on the balls and then wind the yarn over the glue to make designs. Allow the glue to dry before hanging the ornaments around the room.

❀ Spring

Decorated Shamrocks
Let your children use scissors to snip green yarn into tiny pieces. Give the children shamrocks cut from green construction paper. Have them spread glue on the shamrocks and sprinkle the yarn pieces on top of the glue.

☀ Summer

Waves
For each of your children, draw wavy lines on a piece of construction paper. Let the children glue pieces of blue yarn on the lines to make "waves."

Totline® Books

For parents, teachers, and others who work with young children

BEAR HUGS® SERIES

Think you can't make it through another day? Give yourself a Bear Hug! This unique series focuses on positive behavior in young children and how to encourage it on a group and individual level.

Meals and Snacks

Cleanup

Nap Time

Remembering the Rules

Staying in Line

Circle Time

Transition Times

Time Out

Saying Goodbye

Saving the Earth

Getting Along

Fostering Self-Esteem

Being Afraid

Being Responsible

Being Healthy

Welcoming Children

Accepting Change

Respecting Others

1001 SERIES

These super reference books are filled with just the right tip, prop, or poem for your projects.

1001 Teaching Props

1001 Teaching Tips

1001 Rhymes & Fingerplays

THE BEST OF TOTLINE®

A collection of the best ideas from more than a decade's worth of Totline Newsletters. Month-by-month resource guides include instant, hands-on ideas for around-the-curriculum activities. 400 pages

LEARNING & CARING ABOUT SERIES

Developmentally appropriate activities to help children explore, understand, and appreciate the world around them. Includes reproducible parent flyers.

Our World

Our Selves

Our Town

MIX AND MATCH PATTERNS

Simple patterns, each printed in four sizes.

Animal Patterns

Everyday Patterns

Nature Patterns

Holiday Patterns

1•2•3 SERIES

Open-ended, age-appropriate, cooperative, and no-lose experiences for working with preschool children.

1•2•3 Art

1•2•3 Games

1•2•3 Colors

1•2•3 Puppets

1•2•3 Reading & Writing

1•2•3 Rhymes, Stories & Songs

1•2•3 Math

1•2•3 Science

1•2•3 Shapes

101 TIPS FOR DIRECTORS

Great ideas for managing a preschool or daycare! These hassle-free, handy hints help directors juggle the many hats they wear.

Staff and Parent Self-Esteem

Parent Communication

Health and Safety

Marketing Your Center

Resources for You and Your Center

Child Development Training

FOUR SEASONS SERIES

Each book in this delightful series provides fun, hands-on activity ideas for each season of the year.

Four Seasons Movement

Four Seasons Science

A YEAR OF FUN

These age-specific books provide information about how young children are growing and changing and what parents can do to lay a strong foundation for later learning. Calendarlike pages, designed to be displayed, offer developmentally appropriate activity suggestions for each month—plus practical parenting advice!

Just for Babies

Just for One's

Just for Two's

Just for Three's

Just for Four's

Just for Five's

LEARNING EVERYWHERE SERIES

This new series helps parents use everyday opportunities to teach their children. The tools for learning are all around the house and everywhere you go. Easy-to-follow directions show how to combine family fun with learning.

Teaching House

Teaching Town

Teaching Trips

Totline's children's stories are called Teaching Tales because they are two books in one—a storybook and an activity book with fun ideas to expand upon the themes of the story. Perfect for a variety of ages. Each book is written by Jean Warren.

Kids Celebrate the Alphabet

Ellie the Evergreen

The Wishing Fish

The Bear and the Mountain

HUFF AND PUFF® AROUND THE YEAR SERIES

Huff and Puff are two endearing, childlike clouds that will take your children on a new learning adventure each month.

Huff and Puff's Snowy Day

Huff and Puff on Groundhog Day

Huff and Puff's Hat Relay

Huff and Puff's April Showers

Huff and Puff's Hawaiian Rainbow

Huff and Puff Go to Camp

Huff and Puff on Fourth of July

Huff and Puff Around the World

Huff and Puff Go to School

Huff and Puff on Halloween

Huff and Puff on Thanksgiving

Huff and Puff's Foggy Christmas

Totline Books are available at local parent and teacher stores

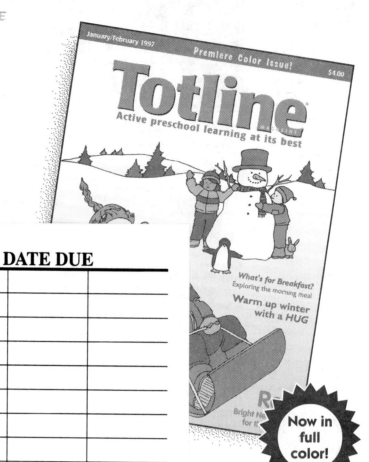

DATE DUE

DEC. 9 1999		
DEC. 0 1999		

Brodart Co.　　　Cat. # 55 137 001　　　Printed in USA

...ngage young children with the ...ive learning in *Totline Magazine*. ...busy, early-childhood profes- ...nts in mind, these activities need ...tion for successful learning fun. ...ssue is perfect for working with ...to six and includes • seasonal ...stories, songs, and rhymes • open-ended art projects and science explorations • reproducible parent pages • ready-made teaching materials • and activities just for toddlers. *Totline Magazine* is the perfect resource for a project-based curriculum in a preschool or at home.

From Totline® Publications